Beautiful America's

Pittsburgh

Published by
Beautiful America Publishing Co.
9725 S.W. Commerce Circle
Wilsonville, Oregon 97070

Library of Congress Cataloging in Publication Data
Beautiful America's Pittsburgh

I. Pittsburgh (Pa.) — Description — Views. I. Kennet, Andrea.
II. Title.   III. Title: Pittsburgh.

F159.P643UT   1987   917.48'86   87-19551

ISBN-0-89802-504-4
ISBN-0-89802-499-4 (Paperback)

Gateway Center Sculpture

Beautiful America's

Pittsburgh

Featuring Walt Urbina Photography
Text by Andrea Kennet

Contents

A Surprising City

Pittsburgh, the nation's most livable city? The hard-muscled city that idolizes the Steelers and Pirates and prefers to order up an "Imp 'n' Arm" (Imperial whisky and Iron City beer) at its blue-collar bars? The city considered to be "a quintessential part of faltering smokestack America," according to one national newspaper? That Pittsburgh?

Aw, come on. The "Smoky City" or the "Rust City," perhaps. Or, as Charles Dickens so colorfully put it, "Hell with the lid taken off."

That was the reaction of many who were taken by surprise when Pittsburgh, Pennsylvania, was named "America's Most Livable City" by the 1985 Rand-McNally "Places Rated Almanac." "Pittsburgh is like Newark without the cultural advantages," joked entertainer Johnny Carson. "I'd rather be a toilet seat in Denver than the mayor of Pittsburgh," sniffed Denver Post columnist Woody Paige, whose city ranked 29th.

But the skeptical, jealous and the surprised who bother to come and look for themselves find an altogether different Pittsburgh than they expected. Not only has Pittsburgh shed the factory soot that gave it a gritty reputation, the city has more character and charm than most large cities. "The fact is, our image is improving dramatically, and any skeptic can be cured with one visit," boasts Mayor Richard S. Caliguiri.

In a report to The New York Times, Lindsey Gruson described the Pittsburgh that first-time visitors can expect:

"The crown of grimy chimneys, which once symbolized this steel town, gave way some years ago to soaring towers, whose skins shimmer at sunrise, beckoning commuters across the Monongahela River like so many sweet sirens. Steel City is now a city of glass. Once a sym-

bol of the industrial region sometimes referred to as the Rust Belt, it is now a renowned health and educational center with a wealth of cultural attractions."

And there's more:

"It's a great Gothic jewel, alive with pinnacles, arches, gargoyles and stained glass. All around, opulence of a bygone era abounds—solid bronze, polished walnut, velvet and gold. There are sumptuous creamy marble spiral staircases and soaring spires that gleam through the night," gushed Jim Powell, a freelancer, in Travel-Holiday.

Brendon Gill, a theater critic for The New Yorker put it more succinctly: "If Pittsburgh were located in Europe, people would travel a thousand miles to visit it."

On the other hand, Pittsburghers were more bemused, than surprised, by the city's ranking. "Pittsburgh seemed to wear the mantle lightly if at all," observes University of Pittsburgh professor and author Samuel Hazo in his "The Pittsburgh That Starts Within You." "Yes, civic leaders and others were euphoric, but the indigenous Pittsburgher shrugged, smiled and went on with his life." Even the Pittsburgh Post-Gazette registered little surprise: "While it is certainly nice that the almanac advances Pittsburgh from fourth (the city's ranking in 1981) to first place, it merely confirms what the locals knew already: That this city has more going for it than going against it."

It's easy to excuse the nonchalant reception to the city's distinction by the 403,000 homefolk. After all, Pittsburgh's beauty is no secret to them. Residents have long maintained a wry chuckle for visitors, who head toward the industrial center without enthusiasm, only to discover urban charm. The city's beauty is a well-kept secret that residents have come to treasure—almost to a fault.

"On behalf of Pittsburgh, I demand a recount," wrote Pittsburgh Post-Gazette columnist Peter Leo in mock alarm. "It's not that we don't deserve to be No. 1. It's just that we're simply not used to being on top in anything that doesn't involve football. Now we have every reason to fear a Yuppie invasion. As you know, Yuppies take lists and ratings very seriously. We don't have enough jogging shoes to go around here."

That joking sentiment isn't one that typifies Pittsburghers. They're very friendly and, in fact, the city takes pride in presenting itself as "The City With a Smile." But a contrasting part of the city's strength—and charm—is that Pittsburgh doesn't really fret about what the rest of the world thinks of it.

Take, for example, the spelling of the city. Any Pittsburgher worth his steel will insist that Pittsburgh with a final "h' is the original and proper spelling, unlike the Pittsburgs of California, Kansas, Illinois or Texas.

The name designation and the "h' were first used by the British general, John Forbes, when he sent notice of victory to William Penn regarding the takeover of Fort Ligonier from the French. On Nov. 27, 1758, he announced the new name of the fort was Fort Pitt and the settlement was "Pittsborough," in honor of England's prime minister.

The final "h' was lost unwillingly when, in a quest for standardization, the United States Board of Geographic Names stripped the final consonant in 1891. Places pronounced "berg" would be spelled "burg," ruled the board. Perseverance among local citizens, who waged a strong battle in legislature, won back the "h' in 1911 when the United States Geographic Board, successor to the geographic names board, voted back the consonant.

Frick Mansion, Point Breeze

Phipps Conservatory, Schenley Park

The "h' is highly regarded by Pittsburghers. "It symbolizes our individuality, our special quality as a city," explains author James Van Trump in an essay about the controversial spelling some years later.

With that same independent spirit, Jonas Salk discovered the vaccine to eradicate polio in Pittsburgh; Robert Fulton launched his first steamboat; George Ferris developed the ferris wheel; Stephen Foster composed scores of songs; and Andrew Carnegie, brothers Andrew and Richard Mellon and others like them pioneered the industry of a surging nation.

Even the city's pro football and baseball teams have the spirit; they've won more championships in six years than in any other American City, to earn Pittsburgh the mantle "City of Champions."

It's that same kind of independent spirit that prompted Pittsburgh to shake off a gritty past to become indeed . . .
BEAUTIFUL PITTSBURGH.

Beautiful Pittsburgh

Nature, as much as anything else, shaped Pittsburgh. Nestled in a valley bordered on the south by 600-foot Mount Washington, where the Allegheny and Monongahela rivers join to form the mighty Ohio, Pittsburgh was well suited as a major shipping point and defense post in early American history. Vast deposits of coal in the nearby Appalachian Mountains helped make the city an industrial force.

Its location at the headwaters of the 987-mile long Ohio River flung Pittsburgh into the midst of three major historic themes: as the target for British dominance of the New World during the French and Indian Wars; then as a focus of activity during the colonies' struggle for independence; and later as the head of the navigation into the vast inland basin during the great migration west.

After its pivotal role in the nation's birth, Pittsburgh settled down to the business of producing steel. By the early 1870's, the city was known as the "forge of the universe," producing half the glass, half the iron and almost all of the oil in the United States. But the metropolis of blast furnaces and belching smokestacks, once considered the "badge of prosperity," spewed out pollution as well as profits. Motorists driving downtown sometimes had to turn on their lights at noon to see through the smog; housewives laundered curtains weekly in an attempt to keep their homes clean and businessmen changed their shirts at mid-day. Pittsburgh developed the image of the "smoky city" that it has devoted more than a century to shed—an image that today is like a black joke without a punchline.

(Opposite) Pittsburgh Regatta from Mt. Washington

Fountain in Point State Park

"With its breathtaking skyline, its scenic waterfront, its cozily vibrant downtown, its rich mixture of cultural and intellectual amenities, its warm neighborhoods and its scrubbed-clean skies, it is no longer the smoky, smelly, gritty milltown of yesteryear," journalist William K. Stevens described the results of the transformation.

The once dominance of heavy industry gave Pittsburgh a virile ambiance that lingers today. "Pittsburgh is masculine," commented Patrick Horsbrugh, in his "Pittsburgh Perceived," a review of the city for Pittsburgh Planning Commission's community renewal program. ". . . its industries set the pace; the buildings commemorate, in four-square strength, the commercial progress of the times. The whole atmosphere is geared to manufacturing, to trading, to education, to things of the future."

Today Pittsburgh is a model of innovation in technology and urban transition as local government, private industry and community cooperate toward a common goal of progress. Pittsburgh is third behind New York and Chicago—and tied with Dallas—as headquarters city for FORTUNE 500 companies. Where steel accounted for upwards of 30 percent of the area's jobs in the late 19th and 20th centuries, today it accounts for just 5 percent as Pittsburgh shifts from a manufacturing to a service economy and forerunner in high technology and research. Yet, Mayor Richard S. Caliguiri cautions, that "much of what Pittsburgh is today—high tech, corporate, clean, affordable and very livable—was built on the backbone of the steel industry, and there is no better backbone on which to build a community."

The Renaissance, as Pittsburgh's first rejuvenation was dubbed, was accomplished quietly, effectively and nearly within a decade. Political prejudices were cast aside. Then-mayor David L. Lawrence, leader of

Pittsburgh at dawn

the Democrats, and Republican leader and banking magnate Richard King Mellon teamed up to lead municipal officials, industry and the community in cleansing the city. Most dramatic was the enactment of the strictest smoke control legislation in the country—predating by 25 years the Federal Clean Air Act—affecting households that heated with coal as well as industry. The law was adopted in 1943 but not put in force until after World War II. Nearly 80 acres of the central business district of railyards, derelict warehouses and outdated machine shops were cleared to make room for 51 new office buildings and some 300 new industries, and construction of expressways. The Gateway Center, the first building completed, remains the premier address for offices, hotels and a condominium tower. At a cost of more than a half million dollars Pittsburgh's original Rennaissance was the most intensive reconstruction of any city in peacetime.

Perhaps the jewel of the project was the development of Point State Park at the apex of the Golden Triangle, as the downtown is called. Its fountain spouts 150 feet skyward and its 36 acres of manicured lawn and gardens and remnants of Fort Pitt reign as the city's symbol where just a few short years ago existed mud, water and commercial sprawl. The park retains some of the past as the site of the original Fort Pitt, named after William Pitt, Earl of Chatham. A six-sided oak block house, built in 1764 and the city's oldest building, and two of the five original bastions—one serves as a museum—have been restored.

That renaissance gave rise in the late 1970's to a second one. "While the steel industry lost buckets of money, seven major buildings were constructed downtown, including a $35 million convention center and Philip Johnson's spectacular $200 million headquarters for PPG Industries. Universities and hospitals attracted companies in computer science, robotics and advanced technologies," reports "Fortune" magazine.

When all the projects already conceived for the downtown are completed, more than 9 million square feet of office space will have been built or newly renovated, and more than 800,000 square feet of retail space, mostly in high fashion and quality dining and drinking establishments, will be added. Perhaps most symbolic of this latest transformation is the 51-acre Pittsburgh Science and Technology Park planned for the former site of a Jones and Laughlin Steel (now LTV Steel) Pittsburgh Works rolling mill on the banks of the Monongahela.

Pushing full steam ahead, in 1985 civic, business and educational leaders announced a $1.9 million economic recovery plan designed to revitalize the decaying steel industry while developing the area as a high technology region. The program, described as "a thrust into the 21st century," will equal in scope the post-World War II renaissance.

At the same time, Pittsburgh isn't turning its back on its past. Much of the city's beauty comes not only from its numerous 100-and 200-year-old buildings, but from the fact that they are used. Horsbrugh was struck by that emphasis on preservation, remarking that part of the city's attractiveness "is one of natural inheritance . . . it survives and is as available as ever for anyone who will pause to perceive."

Four 19th-century churches in downtown are marked historic landmarks and still house worship services. The Allegheny County Courthouse and Jail, a bit reminiscent of a medieval fortress in its late 1800's Romanesque grandeur, is still used for its original purpose. Old street cars operate on the city's new light rail system. When the food processing family, the Heinzes, wanted to give the city a cultural center, it was natural to remodel the old Penn Theater from its rococco obsolesence

PPG Place

(Opposite) Sunset reflections on PPG Building

into Heinz Hall for the Performing Arts, a blending of baroque grandeur and modern acoustics. The city continues to preserve its history with a $150 million renovation of Stanley Theater into the Benedum Center for the Performing Arts. Opened in 1987, it is a major attraction.

An old cemetery in the center of downtown would seem incongruous in any other city. Trinity Burial Ground, located between Trinity Episcopal Cathedral and First Presbyterian Church, is the oldest unreconstructed city landmark. Once a full block with 4,000 graves, progress has whittled away the burial ground to a handful of gravestones and grassy patch between the two 19th-century churches. Once an Indian burial ground and cemetery for the French and British forts, the cemetery is still the resting place of historic figures, including Red Pole, principal chief of the Shawnee nation.

This habit of mixing the old with the new results in some unexpected combinations. The sleek lines of the 64-story USX (formerly U.S. Steel) building, tallest between Chicago and New York when erected in 1970, shares the horizon with the gingerbread facade of the old Union Trust building. The Alcoa Building, America's first aluminium skyscraper, rivals for attention with the black open-metal steeple of the Old Smithfield Congregational Church built in 1925.

Even the physical setting of the city presents a contrast of pictures. From the north, the rural entry provides an idyllic setting. Travelers from the south are startled with a sudden, breathtaking view of the Golden Triangle as they emerge from the Fort Pitt Tunnel. The masculinity of the city permeates the eastern entry along the momentous Monongahela, passing remnants of old steelmills. The Ohio River opens from a tranquil, leisurely pace beneath the West End Bridge to reveal the port city.

In an acrobatic twist, Pittsburgh manages to turn around an old adage and balance a haystack on top of a needle. Concentrated in the half-mile square Golden Triangle, heart of the city, are major corporate headquarters and employment, education, dining, shopping and entertainment easily within walking distance to suit a metropolitan population of 2.4 million people. The close proximity of work and culture makes Pittsburgh a city on its feet, literally. Once downtown, either by trolley, bus, subway or private vehicle, everything a person could desire is at hand, or at foot.

The rivers pour life into Pittsburgh. Aptly described as "the city (that) rises out of the rivers," by a local newspaper, Pittsburgh relies on the rivers as its economic and recreational lifeblood. The rivers crown Pittsburgh as the nation's largest inland port. Tugboats power barges of coal and other raw materials to points across the nation. Those same waterways support the annual Three Rivers Regatta, featuring Formula I boat racing, ski shows and other festivites.

The Allegheny River, its Indian name meaning "Stream of the Cave People," provides the arena for most of the recreational boating. Industry freight travels the Monongahela, "high banks falling down" in Indian and "The Mon" among local folks. Barges ply the Ohio, whose name comes from a Delaware word meaning "white with frothing water."

The need to ford the rivers prompted Pittsburgh to build bridges, some 720 of them, to earn the city the label of "city of bridges." And, there are another 1,300 in Allegheny County, more perhaps than any other place except Venice.

Major tunnels pierce the hillsides to give access from the suburbs to downtown. Two inclines, relics of the past, continue to operate, in part because of people's affections for them and because residents rely on them as alternate transportation to the top of Mount Washington.

Oxford Building

Oxford Center

Lunch at Oxford Center

25

The Golden Triangle

Shrewd forethought overruled a minority desire to build Fort Pitt at McKees Rocks, where the Ohio Company of Virginia had started erecting the original outpost in early 1754. The French, who seized the fort two months later, foresaw the Point as a more strategic position—a sentiment expressed just the year before by 21-year-old George Washington. The British army, which captured old Fort Duquesne and renamed it Fort Pitt, agreed.

Ever since, land at the confluence of the two rivers, the Golden Triangle-as it was first proclaimed by the "Saturday Evening Post" in 1914-has served as the heart and symbol of Pittsburgh. It is the Point that inspired the phrase "I am smith of land and sea," and the steel industry, the strain, "monarch of all the forges," in the 19th-century Hymn of Pittsburgh by Richard Realt.

First, it was a shipping port for the farms and then for the industry that sprang up rapidly after the War of 1812. In the mid-1800's as Pittsburgh turned in its plows for steel forges, the Golden Triangle took on a new look with increased production and population. Accomplishments were many, but the result gave English author Charles Dickens the impression of "an ugly confusion of backs of buildings and crazy galleries and stairs."

The Point has always been the focus of the half-mile square city center, both for its beauty and its navigational advantages. It is natural that Point State Park and its fountain, fed by a fourth mysterious underground river, basks in favor of both visitors and residents. The 36-acre park at the apex offers passive recreation, concerts, festivals and beautiful vistas of the Three Rivers, the downtown skyline and the surrounding hills.

But the Point only begins the conglomeration of business and industry, churches and residences, restaurants, theaters and entertainment places that jostle each other for room and attention in the triangle.

At the eastern end of the park and across Commonwealth Avenue is Gateway Center, the site where the first Renaissance began in the 1950's. Eastward along Liberty Avenue past another Renaissance original, Equitable Plaza gardens, rise the Oliver Plaza buildings, more current accomplishments.

Just one block southeast, on Sixth Avenue, two monarchs of established religion dramatically contrast the modern Oliver Plaza and Gateway Center. The First Presbyterian Church and Trinity Episcopal Cathedral fence in the Old Trinity Burial Ground where many of Pittsburgh's pioneers rest.

East on Sixth are more city landmarks that illustrate how architecture of other times coexists in Pittsburgh. Mellon Square is bordered on one side by the Alcoa building. The 31-story, 410-foot tall structure, built in 1952, was the world's first aluminum skyscraper; only the structure's frame is steel. Surrounding buildings illustrate other construction styles of passing popularity—The William Penn Hotel and Union Trust Co. Building, both old and ornate, stand next to the modern Mellon Bank Building. The USX Tower rises 64 stories, further east on Sixth.

Steel Plaza Station, the hub of the light rail transit subway system, connects 15 miles of south neighborhoods to downtown. Opened in 1985, the system fulfilled a 60-year dream for a subway system in Pittsburgh.

Southward from the steel headquarters stand the imposing and massive Allegheny County Courthouse and Jail, squatting over two blocks at Grant and Forbes. Described by "Travel-Holiday" magazine as a "fortress of justice," the Romanesque buildings are the last work of the great 19th-century American architect Henry Hobson Richardson, who also designed Boston's Trinity Church.

Grant Street is Pittsburgh's "money street," transformed by the surging Renaissance II with the construction of several new buildings, including the symbol of this second revival, PPG Place. Fanciful and fun to look at, the 1.7 million-square-foot shimmering cathedral is sheathed with almost 50 acres of reflective glass. The six buildings of the complex, topped with 231 spires, surround a block-sized public square. Dubbed the crystal palace by locals for its resemblance to a medieval cathedral, the neo-Gothic glass quadrangle designed by Philip Johnson houses shops, restaurants and the headquarters of the Fortune 500 glass and paintmaker PPG Industries, formerly Pittsburgh Plate Glass.

"Folds of glass result in a dazzling interplay of light and shadow. It glows with a blush of color at dawn, sparkles like crystal during the day and assumes a burnt orange blaze by sunset. It's the highlight of Pittsburgh's evening skyline," declares freelance writer Jim Powell in "Travel-Holiday" magazine.

Nearby are the twin towers of One Mellon Bank and One Oxford Center. The two 46-story towers flow into a public urban plaza.

Pittsburgh's Golden Triangle is indeed booming like never before. Close to completion, more than 9 million square feet of office space has been constructed or newly renovated, and 800,000 square feet of retail space, mostly in ultra fashions and gourmet dining and drinking emporiums added.

Other recent accomplishments of the second Renaissance are the David Lawrence Convention Center, Liberty Center, Chatham Center II, Consolidated Natural Gas Tower and Hillman Building.

Completion of the $137 million Liberty Center hotel, offices and commercial complex is expected to spur development of the Strip District and other adjacent areas. Long home to the region's produce distribution yards, the Strip District now integrates retail food, restaurant and gourmet foods businesses as well.

An old farmer's market area further west on Forbes has been turned into Market Square, a block of greenery and fountain, yet another break from downtown concrete. Heinz Hall, cultural center of Pittsburgh and home of its music, stands at Penn Avenue and Sixth. The Pittsburgh Symphony performs to packed houses amid a plush interior adorned with Breche opal, Levanto marble, red velvet, sparkling crystal and gold leaf. A $150 million renovation of Stanley Theater into the Benedum Center for the Performing Arts provides a permanent new home for the Pittsburgh Opera, Civic Light Opera and Pittsburgh Ballet Theater.

Flag Plaza, in the Lower Hill area, is home to the local council of the Boy Scouts of America and the National Flag Foundation. It is one of few sites in the nation where the U.S. flag is allowed to fly 24 hours a day.

Across the street is the Civic Arena, which features the world's largest retractable domed roof. It is "home ice" to the Pittsburgh Penguins, a National Hockey League team.

The four-time Super Bowl champion Pittsburgh Steelers football team and the former world champion Pirates baseball team share Three Rivers Stadium, on the north shore of the Allegheny across from the Point. When both teams won their championships in 1979-80, Pittsburgh enjoyed a brief reign as "the City of Champions".

A science and technology center with Omnimax theater, a children's museum based on "Mister Roger's Neighborhood" (a television program produced in Pittsburgh), a technology market place for business, hotels, retail shops and parking are envisioned by the city planning department for the area near Three Rivers Stadium.

Industry shares the waters of the Allegheny River, popular with pleasure craft. Pittsburgh's many bridges provide a myriad of spectacular sights. One of the most breath-taking is the "Trilogy of Bridges," composed of the Sixth, Seventh and Ninth street bridges, all self-anchored I-bar suspension bridges with center spans that exceed 400 feet and stretch more than 1,200 feet in length.

The North Shore Complex, located near Three Rivers Stadium, illustrates how the city's Golden Triangle is evolving into the "Golden Circle."

America's love affair with railroads is evident at Station Square. Located across the Smithfield Bridge, over the Monongahela River, from the Golden Triangle, Station Square is a festive marketplace of more than 70 shops and restaurants in the restored Pittsburgh & Lake Erie Railroad freight house, built in 1910 when railroads were the gateway to the city. The vaulted Victorian rotunda, ornate iron work and brick walkways provide a grand setting.

Grand Steps, Carnegie Museum

Pre-Historic Times, Carnegie Museum

The Tightrope Walker, Carnegie Museum

"Four arched corner turrets suggest entrances to mysterious caverns," says James D. Van Trump, a champion of Pittsburgh architecture. "There is implicit in the general composition the imperial, tenebrous architectural visions of Piranesi, or the haunting classical nostalgia of Hubert Robert."

Displayed on a spotlighted stage like a fine sculpture is a black Bessemer convert from an old steel mill. Old locomotives and passenger cars recall the days when trains transformed our nation.

Providing yet another memory is the Gateway Clipper Riverboat Fleet that offers scenic rides on the Three Rivers from the north shore of the Monongahela.

Neighborhoods

Early Pittsburghers had to look no further than the coal-fired melting pots of their steel and glass mills for a metaphor to describe the population of their rapidly-growing industrial city. The melting pot syndrome hit Pittsburgh just before the 20th century. Early residents shared the same European cultural backgrounds, immigrating mostly to the southwestern Pennsylvania metropolis from Scotland, Wales, Ireland, Germany and England. But an immigration wave in the 1880's brought groups of quite different origins. Arriving with high hopes to work in the glass factories, steel mills and coal mines were Hungarians, Poles, Estonians, Latvians, Czechs, Greeks and Armenians.

Those early ethnic roots are visible today throughout the city. Neighborhoods with stores and residential mailboxes bearing names of particular nationalities illustrate the tendency of similar cultures to settle together. Old religions and customs survive "Americanization". For instance, a half dozen Catholic churches located within a few blocks of each other may be close in proximity but differ in the nationalities they serve: Ukrainian, Bulgarian or Italian. Some radio stations broadcast programs varying from Hebrew, Polish, Italian and Greek, to the more exotic tongues of Croatian, Lithuanian, Serbian and Slovenian. Festivals celebrate the different heritages and share the good times with others. Each year, a green stripe down certain streets announces St. Patrick's Day on March 17, when the Irish and just about everybody else pay tribute to the patron saint of Ireland.

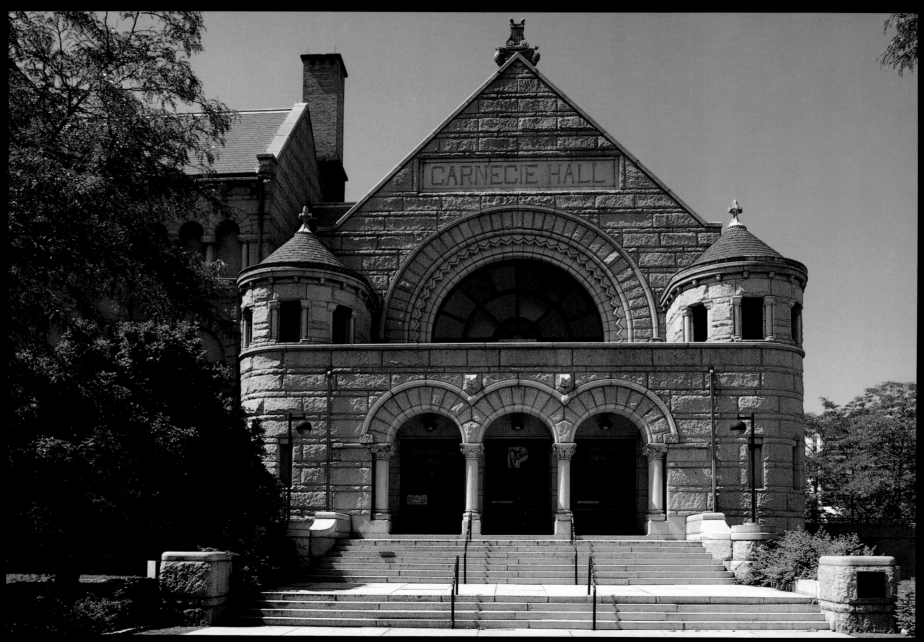

Carnegie Hall, Pittsburgh's Public Theater

Old Post Office Building, now a Children's Museum at Landmark Square

Much of the tight-knit community style exists today. Pittsburgh boasts of 88 solid neighborhoods, like Squirrel Hill, Highland Park, South Side and Troy Hill, to name a few.

Realizing the riches the neighborhoods offer, city leaders have devoted the bulk of Renaissance II's capital improvement budget to improving housing, commercial areas, streets, utilities and parks in all neighborhoods. "Neighborhood revitalization is an equal goal with economic development," vows Mayor Richard S. Caliguiri, who has been credited as the spark behind the revival of the Renaissance movement.

That awareness is described in a "Travel Holiday's Profile on Pittsburgh," which quotes Arthur Ziegler: "As the old and familar facades crashed down to the thunderous beat of wrecking balls, there was a growing awareness that in certain areas of this historic city, which dates back to 1758, many buildings and entire neighborhoods are worth preserving. If they were allowed to vanish, they'd take with them Pittsburgh's living memory of itself."

East

Two neighborhoods east of the Golden Triangle present a great contrast. The Hill area, nestled between downtown and Oakland, struggles against the blight of substandard housing. It contains remarkable, albeit decaying, relics of 19th-century row-housing and tenements. But despite its appearance, the community thrives with social interaction and life.

Pittsburgh's cultural life flourishes in Oakland, a few blocks up the slope from the Hill. Its residential section claims a moneyed past and was hailed in 1899 as "the most beautiful suburb in the world," by an immodest Pittsburgh Board of Trade. The spacious and popular Schenley Park is here.

And, it is here that Carnegie, Mellon and others endowed their libraries, museums and universities. Oakland has become the center of Pittsburgh's medical research and high-technology development.

Two major research universities, Carnegie-Mellon and the University of Pittsburgh, are situated here. Oakland is also the medical center of the region that includes Presbyterian University Hospital, the principal organ transplant hospital in the world. Also located here is the largest and most advanced nuclear magnetic resonance facility in the world. A biotechnology manufacturing park at the Universtiy of Pittsburgh will make it the most advanced biomedical research facility, continuing a tradition that resulted in the Salk polio vaccines, synthetic insulin and synthetic protein—all developed in Pittsburgh.

Carnegie-Mellon University, nationally reputed as one of the finest

A shimmering, and growing Pittsburgh skyline

Pittsburgh on a clear winter night

technical research universities, is at the forefront of robotic development and was the first university to computerize every system. It recently landed a U.S. Defense Department contract to house the software engineering institute.

New life has been breathed into East Liberty to restore the neighborhood to its former postion as the hub of the city's East End. Grass roots organizations at town hall meetings demanded—and got—a comprehensive renewal program, giving the community the status as the "neighborhood that dared." The Omego Street Group, a loosely organized group of 11 property owners who trace their origins to the same Italian hamlet, exemplified the local struggle against the odds to keep neighborhoods intact hand-in-hand with urban renewal. The Omego Group slowly acquired and rehabilitated rundown properties with assistance from government agencies.

South

Across the Monongahela River, southwest from downtown, lies some of the city's most traditionally desired real estate and historic land. Homestead once was a separate city spawned by the Bessemer Steel Plant. A splendid view of downtown and the rivers from atop Mount Washington gives properties further west a special status. Village-like communities cover the slope between South Side and Allentown on Mount Oliver, similar to those on Mount Washington where some wonderful restaurants share the view. Each of the communities has a common design with their identity spelled through the principal feature of the neighborhood—the churches.

Southside, a little older, retains its grace against the more magnificent homes on Mount Washington and Mount Oliver. Narrow stairs, row houses and cobblestone roads give Southside a special character. Onion-shaped steeples, rather than the spires that top traditional American churches, reflect the Hungarian and Bulgarian ancestry of residents. Houses and other buildings huddle close to each other. Old though the neighborhoods are, residents proudly maintain their homes and streets.

Duquesne University overlooks the commerce center from "The Bluff."

Mount Washington overlooks downtown Pittsburgh and the Three Rivers. The Monongahela and Duquesne inclines, railcars dating back to 1870, are a charming reminder of old-fashioned ways, like San Francisco's cable cars. The cars of hand carved cherry panels with bird's

County Courthouse, One Mellon Bank Building and USX Building

County Courthouse

Civic Arena

eye maple trim accomodate 12 people and provide a spectacular vista of the city below.

A little further out are the neighborhoods of Greentree, Mount Lebanon and Castle Shannon, each similar to other Pittsburgh communities but at the same time, each with individual traits that make them so unique.

West of downtown along the Ohio River is McKees Rocks, housing a mixture of ethnic heritages. For centuries, the hills were an Indian burial ground and cover three layers of burial sites dating from 3000 B.C. to 1500 A.D.

Stephen Foster Monument

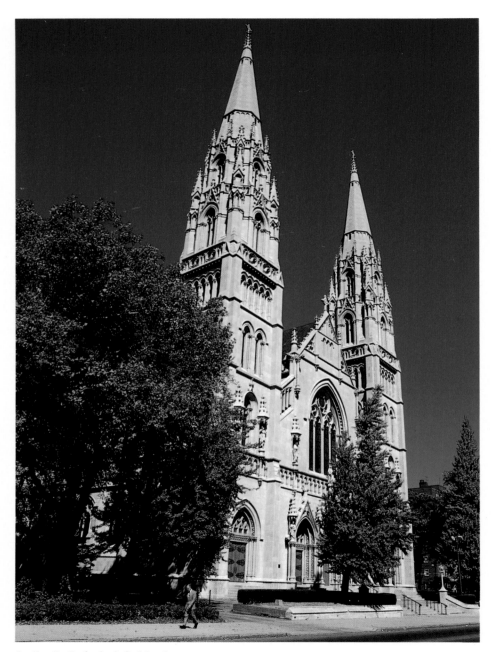

St. Paul's Cathedral, Oakland

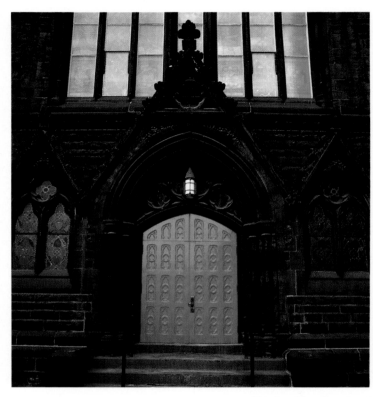

Trinity Church at Sixth

Holy Spirit Catholic Byzantine Rites Church, Oakland

Heinz Hall for the Performing Arts

Heinz Hall Plaza

University of Pittsburgh, Heinz Chapel

Cathedral of Learning, University of Pittsburgh

One of the contestants

Three Rivers Arts Festival

Three Rivers Stadium, The Point and the bridges

Oxford, Mellon and USX Buildings in afternoon sun

The Workers Sculpture, NorthShore Center

Three Rivers Stadium

Equitable Plaza, Gateway Center

©Pittsburgh Steelers

(Opposite) The Pittsburgh Pirates

Pittsburgh Three Rivers Regatta

The Pittsburgh Marathon

Old Allegheny/North Side

Much sentimental and historic attachment are connected with North Side, which spreads from the shores of the Ohio and Allegheny rivers to the inland hills. The idiomatic "North Side" hardly describes the color and position once held by the area that encompasses the former city of Allegheny and its neighborhoods. Residents understandably abhor the name North Side, considering it to lower Allegheny's status to an appendage to Pittsburgh.

Annexed by Pittsburgh in 1907, Allegheny and its surrounding colorful neighborhoods hosted some of the area's more elegant and gracious living until its decline in the 1900's. The area typifies late 19th-century residential neighborhoods that developed in many industrial cities and deteriorated through the mid-20th century. Society Hill is now home to a community college, in contrast to the leisure life it once nurtured.

North Side's Old Allegheny encompasses neighborhoods unique in their identities: North Shore, Old Allegheny's riverfront; Central North Side, the heart of Old Allegheny and its commons; East North Side, once Dutchtown, a commercial center where German and English were both taught in public schools until 1925; Allegheny West and its remarkable townhouses; Manchester, once a solid upper-class suburb; Perry Hilltop and Fineview, with beautiful yards and views; and Troy Hill and its German village layout.

Pittsburgh's ethnic heritage is best illustrated in Allegheny. English descendants settled in Old Allegheny town with the Commons; Scots and Irish lived westward in Manchester. Germans settled eastward in Dutchtown at the southern end of East Street. Germans also inhabited inland areas and the Swiss lived in Swiss Hole by the Allegheny shores.

The architecture of the area is as varied and interesting as the city itself, ranging from Federal style and Greek Revival pediment and pilaster works seen on the Old Widows Home on Armandale, to the pretentious Italianate style of Manchester or Perry Hilltop. Stained glass, often Tiffany, turrets and ornate facades turn plain brick box-like houses into works of art.

Old Allegheny conjures one of the largest nostalgic lump in the throats of oldtimers. Organized several years after Pittsburgh's founding in 1759, Allegheny was slow to mature chiefly because of frequent Indian traffic in the area and because of a strange twist in claims by Pennsylvania and Virginia to the Pittsburgh area until Congress resolved the issue after the American Revolution. The area was part of a 3,000-acre reservation tract to meet the state's obligations to its war veterans.

Incorporated in 1840, Allegheny boasted all of the amenities of early urban living through such institutions as Allegheny Market house, Boggs and Buhl department store, Ober Park and its magnificent fountain, Lake Elizabeth, the Music Hall of Allegheny Library and the Heinz plant. The University of Pittsburgh opened here in 1882 at Buena Vista and Perrysville before moving to Oakland in 1900.

Much of the old grandeur is gone, but efforts are being taken to recapture and rejuvenate the former city's status and beauty. The deteriorating row houses are marked for restoration. Assisted by a city

grant, the North Side Civic Properties Corp. transformed a derelict warehouse into industrial space, called 1000 California Avenue, that is fully rented. Some of the buildings from the old commons remain, thanks to the Pittsburgh Historic and Landmarks Foundation. Standing out in the mixture of modern stores, professional buildings and parking garages at Allegheny Center is the Old Post Office Museum. The city post office for many years, it is now a children's museum and headquarters for the historical foundation.

Allegheny Center was built on the site of the old Allegheny commons in an effort to restore both the city and its spirit. The Old Post Office, Market Square and the first Carnegie Public Library share the new commons.

Four distinct neighborhoods remain intact abutting the Allegheny Commons on the north, west and east. Central North Side has been the most stable community and has been revitalized to a great degree. The Mexican War Streets on the other side of West Park were designated as the city's original historic district. Laid out around 1850, the street names are associated with the war that was then current. Like surrounding communities, the Mexican War Streets were built by the industrial rich and reflect the individual builder's tastes. The homes were gradually converted into rooming houses as the upper-income residents moved east and north to the suburbs in the early 1900's. Today it is a quiet, elegant urban neighborhood of turn-of-the-century townhouses within walking distance of the downtown.

Two other North Side historic neighborhoods, Manchester and Allegheny West are also witnessing striking renovations of historic housing. Filled with mid-and late-Victorian houses, Allegheny West is of similiar date and character to Central North Side. Manchester, just west of Allegheny West, sports sprawling lawns compared to the tight, brick housing of Allegheny. New styles and larger lawns spawned some Italian Villa and Queen Anne architecture. The area was built in 1860 first by Jewish merchants and then German businessmen.

Perry Hilltop, overlooking central Allegheny is a chain of neighborhoods strung together along Perrysville Avenue. Some structures date as far back as 1850 but the majority were built in 1900 when trolley service started. Some of the best samples of Colonial Revival houses dress Perrysville Avenue. Nearby Fineview and East Street Valley are similar in grid-plan design and architecture.

Troy Hill, settled in the mid 19th-century, is a compact, stable community with the aura of a medieval hill town, and is still predominately German Catholic. Spring Hill, between Troy Hill and East Street, is another mostly German community, with housing dating from 1850 to 1920.

PPG Building

Market Square

(Opposite) PPG Arts Festival

City Of Benefactors

Pittsburgh's wealthy and prominent haven't forgotten their city. Their generosity is perhaps most evident in Oakland, where Carnegie, Mellon and others endowed libraries, museums and universities.

The area's most prominent landmark may be the 42-story Cathedral of Learning at the University of Pittsburgh. Started during the 1920's as what has been described as "a Gothic fantasy," it has 18 classrooms, each in a distinctive national style, celebrating the city's ethnic traditions. Pittsburgh's wealthy collected some unusual "items," and in this Cathedral is a Greek-Revival ballroom from the 1835 Schenley mansion and an 18th-century library from Damascus. To ensure the building's completion during the Great Depression, the University had the Cathedral literally built from the top down. When construction faltered, the cash-strapped University got contributions by selling bricks to 97,000 shoolchildren and 17,000 adults.

Nearby stands the Carnegie Library, housing some 2.2 million volumes, that was donated to the city by Andrew Carnegie. As the story goes, Carnegie recalled his penniless years of borrowing books and endowed some 2,000 free libraries so that others could improve themselves through reading.

The Carnegie Music Hall houses one of the world's largest organs; each of its 8,600 pipes is 32 inches long and weighs 1,000 pounds. The Carnegie Architecture Hall features life-size models of artifacts such as the tomb of Mausolus of Halicarnassus in Asia, the Parthenon of Athens and the 12th-century Romanesque Church of St. Gilles du Gard, Frances.

A wide range of American art can be viewed at the Sarah Mellon Scaife Gallery at the Carnegie Institute, while Henry Clay Frick's love of the Old Master paintings is apparent at the Frick Art Museum. Carnegie Museum of Natural History supports three floors of 10,000 exhibits ranging across all fields of natural history and anthropology.

Those with a fancy for plants will enjoy "green-thumbing" through fine botanical prints from medieval times to the present day at the Hunt Institute for Botanical Documentation at the the Carnegie-Mellon University. Or, make a relaxing visit to the Phipps Conservatory, a gift of Henry Phipps who was a partner with Andrew Carnegie, to view its 64,000 plant specimens from around the world in 13 greenhouses.

Another tradition firmly ingrained in Pittsburgh is the development of parks. Most are the result of the same philanthropic bent that feed the educational and cultural communitities. The local folk seem to appreciate the gifts; parks seem to be used at all hours, as is the downtown, reflecting a yen for the advantages of urban life and a desire for nature.

Pittsburgh parks share a common scheme of broad lawns, clipped and manicured, splashes of flower beds, cozy groves of deciduous trees, and the inevitable fountains and statues. Roadways curve through many of the parks, and walking paths meander through the greenery. Yet, each park retains a sense of individuality.

Schenley Park, abutting the University of Pittsburgh and Carnegie Mellon University in Oakland, is perhaps the most spectacular of the city parks. Its wide variety of attractions makes Schenley Park a popular spot for residents and visitors alike. It is home for the Phipps Conservatory, a nature museum, golf course, hiking trails and tennis courts. The view from the top of the hill in the park affords a splendid

Manchester

Mexican War Street

panorama of the city, three rivers and many hills—a wonderful place to watch the sun set over the city. Panther Hollow Lake in Schenley Park recalls a hunt organized in the 1760's to drive out a feared panther.

Pittsburgh profited when 15-year-old Mary Grohan, granddaughter of wealthy capitalist James O'Hara eloped with soldier Capt. Edward Schenley, twice widowed and nearly thrice his bride's age. Her controversial marrige to the poorer, older man split the family. After Mrs. Schenley reclaimed her estate through a lawsuit, she donated 300 acres in Oakland in 1889 for a park. She also gave the aged block house on Point State Park to the Daughters of the American Revolution.

A short drive east to Squirrel Hill— a neighborhood named for an abundance of that critter—is Frick Park. It is a contrast to other city parks because of its emphasis on nature and wilderness, which is unmarred by roadways.

Along the north shore of the Allegheny River stretches Roberto Clemente Memorial Park, a natural gathering spot for river watchers and pilots of pleasure craft. The park ends just short of Three River Stadium.

Further north and west is Riverside Park, where stargazers get a heavenly view of the skies through a 116-foot telescope at the whitedomed Allegheny Observatory. Allegheny Center's Buhl Planetarium presents a host of science and space exhibitions. Perrys Athletic Field, adjacent to the park, offers sporting events. Nearby Pittsburgh Aviary is home to more than 200 species of birds, which live in a large free flight environment.

North Park and South Park are enormous dedications of public open space that are appropriately named for their locations from the downtown.

In 1984, the city dedicated its first urban sculpture park as part of the North Shore Center redevelopment project. Allegheny Landing on the